FILTERS FOR
THE MIND

BY CHAD LEHTONEN

**Edited masterfully by Yuan Li Lehtonen,
along with insightful contributions from
my mom, Linda Lehtonen.**

INTROSPECTIVE FOOD
FOR THOUGHT

EVEN THE GREATEST JOURNEY STARTS WITH JUST ONE SINGLE STEP.

OTHER PRINCIPLES ARE FOLLOWED
BY OTHER PEOPLE. ALWAYS LIVE BY
YOUR OWN PRINCIPLES.

PEOPLE SEE WHAT THEY WANT TO SEE AND HEAR WHAT THEY WANT TO HEAR. DON'T FALL INTO THAT TRAP. ALWAYS KEEP YOUR EYES AND EARS WIDE OPEN.

DON'T BE A SLAVE TO SOCIETY. BE TRUE TO YOURSELF.

IT'S IMPORTANT TO RESPECT YOUR FATHER. IT'S MORE IMPORTANT TO RESPECT YOURSELF, YOUR OPINIONS, AND YOUR DECISIONS, EVEN IF THEY ARE CONTRARY TO HIS.

HONESTY IS ALWAYS THE BEST POLICY. TRYING TO REMEMBER ALL OF THE LIES THAT ONE'S TOLD IS IMPOSSIBLE.

USE YOUR WIT TO AMUSE AND NOT TO ABUSE.

OWNING CATS IS THERAPEUTIC.
THEY'RE FULL OF CHARACTER AND
LOVE AND WATCHING THEM EAT
CATNIP IS MORE ENTERTAINING THAN
MOST TV SHOWS.

IF YOU DECIDE TO HESITATE, YOU PROBABLY SHOULDN'T DO IT. INTUITION HAS KEPT PEOPLE ALIVE SINCE THE START OF TIME.

WHEN GRIEVING THE LOSS OF A LOVED
ONE, DON'T FORGET TO CONSIDER
HOW THEY WOULD WANT YOU TO GO
ON WITH YOUR LIFE GOING FORWARD.

IT'S IMPORTANT TO PASS ON YOUR
WISDOM AND YOUR LIFE'S LESSONS TO
YOUR LOVED ONES.

PEOPLE WHO JUDGE OTHERS RELY ON USING GUILT. IT HELPS KEEP THEM FROM HAVING TO DEAL WITH THEIR OWN FEELINGS OF GUILT.

YOU DON'T MAKE YOURSELF BETTER
BY BRAGGING. YOU MAKE YOURSELF
BETTER BY ACHIEVING AND BEING
HUMBLE ABOUT IT.

WHENEVER LIFE GETS TOO
COMPLICATED, DO YOUR BEST TO
MAKE IT SIMPLE.

SOME PEOPLE CAN FIX ALMOST ANYTHING, BUT THEY CAN'T FIX 'CRAZY'.

"LET IT BE. THERE WILL ALWAYS BE AN ANSWER, LET IT BE." -PAUL MCCARTNEY

WHEN YOU FEEL THAT ALL ARROWS
ARE POINTED AGAINST YOU, THERE IS
ALWAYS A LIGHT AT THE END OF THE
TUNNEL. YOU JUST HAVE TO LOOK TO
SEE IT.

RESPECT YOUR ELDERS. THEY DESERVE IT AND THEY HAVE A LIFETIME OF KNOWLEDGE AND EXPERIENCE TO SHARE.

NEVER LET YOUR EGO OVERRIDE YOUR BRAIN.

THE VERY BEST FRIEND THAT YOU'VE GOT IN THIS WORLD IS YOU.

THE ABILITY TO BE LOVED IS ONLY A POSSIBILITY WHEN YOU ARE ABLE TO LOVE YOURSELF.

ONE OF THE SECRETS TO BEING
HUMBLE IS HAVING THE ABILITY TO
LISTEN.

BODY LANGUAGE SPEAKS LOUDER THAN ANY SPECIFIC LANGUAGE.

NOBODY PROMISED US A TOMORROW.
YOU'VE GOT TO TAKE LIFE AS IT
COMES.

WHEN IT COMES TO YOUR CHILDREN, WHETHER YOU APPROVE OF THEM OR NOT, YOU MUST LOVE THEM UNCONDITIONALLY. EVERY CHILD DESERVES LOVE AND RESPECT FROM THEIR PARENTS. LOVE YOUR CHILDREN.

DON'T BE AFRAID OF WHAT YOU
BELIEVE IN YOUR HEART. THERE'S
MORE TRUTH IN THERE THAN YOU'LL
EVER FIND IN YOUR MIND.

THOSE WHO DON'T LEARN FROM THE MISTAKES OF HISTORY WILL EVENTUALLY REPEAT THEM.

WHEN YOUR TROUBLES BECOME
OVERWHELMING, JUST IMAGINE THAT
YOU'RE FLOATING UP IN THE SKY
LOOKING DOWN ON THE
NEIGHBORHOOD AND REALIZE THAT A
LOT OF THE PROBLEMS IN THE
SURROUNDING HOUSES OUTWEIGH
YOURS. PERSPECTIVE IS KEY.

YOU'RE GOING TO MEET A LOT OF
PEOPLE IN YOUR LIFE. SOME OF THEM
YOU'LL LIKE, AND SOME OF THEM YOU
WON'T. IT SHOULD HAVE NOTHING TO
DO WITH THEIR RACE OR RELIGION,
JUST ABOUT WHO THEY ARE AS A
PERSON.

HOW DO YOU EAT AN ELEPHANT? ONE BITE AT A TIME.

YOU DON'T BECOME A SUCCESS BY
WINNING ALL OF THE TIME. YOU
BECOME A SUCCESS BY LEARNING
HOW TO HANDLE YOUR DEFEATS AND
BY NOT GIVING UP.

YOU ONLY GET ONE RUN THROUGH
LIFE. YOU DON'T GET DO-OVERS. WHY
GO THROUGH LIFE BEING MISERABLE?

THERE ARE THREE KINDS OF PEOPLE IN THIS WORLD. THOSE WHO CAN COUNT, AND THOSE WHO CAN'T.

LET YOUR CHILDREN HOLD ON TO
THEIR INNOCENCE AND IMAGINATION
AS LONG AS THEY CAN.

THREE RULES FOR BEING IN A FIGHT:

1. HIT FIRST AND HIT HARD.
2. EVEN IF YOU'RE NOT,
   PRETEND TO BE BRAVE.
3. NEVER QUIT.

THE MORE THAT WE LEARN ABOUT
EACH OTHER'S RELIGIONS, THE MORE
THAT WE LEARN ABOUT HOW MUCH
WE ARE ALL THE SAME.

WHEN YOU TALK ABOUT YOURSELF, YOU'RE AN IDIOT. WHEN YOU TALK ABOUT ME, YOU'RE A GENIUS!

PASSIVE-AGGRESSIVENESS NEVER WORKS. YOU NEED TO FACE YOUR PROBLEMS HEAD ON.

RESPECT IS EARNED, NOT DESERVED.

A MAN WITH ONE FOOT IN THE PAST
AND ONE FOOT IN THE FUTURE PISSES
ON THE PRESENT.

I WANT TO LIVE IN A PLACE WHERE
KINDNESS IS CONSIDERED A
STRENGTH, NOT A WEAKNESS.

IF YOU DON'T CHANGE YOUR DIRECTION, YOU MAY WIND UP WHERE YOU'RE HEADING.

HOLDING ON TO ANGER IS LIKE
HOLDING ON TO A HOT COAL WITH
THE INTENT OF THROWING IT AT
SOMEONE ELSE. YOU ARE THE ONLY
ONE WHO GETS BURNED.

USE YOUR OWN COMPASS WHEN IT COMES TO UNDERSTANDING WHAT'S GOING ON IN THE NEWS.

WHEN YOU LOOK BACK ON YOUR LIFE
WHILE YOU'RE SITTING IN YOUR
ROCKING CHAIR, YOU'LL REGRET THE
THINGS THAT YOU DIDN'T DO MORE
THAN THE ONES THAT YOU DID.

AN EIGHTY-NINE-YEAR-OLD FEMALE
PATIENT WHO I SAW DURING MY
FIRST WEEK OF BEING AN
OPTOMETRIST TOLD ME THREE RULES
TO LEAD A HAPPY LIFE:

1. HAVE SOMEONE TO
   LOVE AND TO LOVE
   YOU BACK WHETHER
   IT'S A PERSON OR AN
   ANIMAL.
2. BE FINANCIALLY
   STABLE. AS LONG AS
   YOU CAN PAY YOUR
   BILLS, YOU'LL BE
   OKAY.
3. ALWAYS HAVE
   SOMETHING TO LOOK
   FORWARD TO.

I GAVE HER A BIG HUG BEFORE SHE
LEFT AND SAID, "THANK YOU." SHE
DIED SHORTLY THERE-AFTERWARDS.
I WILL NEVER FORGET HER ADVICE.

ALL FAMILIES HAVE PROBLEMS BEHIND CLOSED DOORS. YOURS ISN'T THE ONLY ONE.

BEING MARRIED TO A SPOUSE WHO DOESN'T MIND WHEN YOU TAKE A NAP IS THE GREATEST. BEING MARRIED TO A SPOUSE WHO VACUUMS BESIDE THE COUCH WHILE YOU'RE SLEEPING ON IT SUCKS.

A DAY FILLED WITH LAUGHTER IS A DAY WORTH CHERISHING.

MODERATION IS KEY.

THE BEST WAY TO AVOID A CONFRONTATION IS TO STEP AWAY FROM THE FIGHT.

WHEN YOU SWEAT THE SMALL STUFF, YOU LOSE SIGHT OF THE BIGGER PICTURE. THE BIGGER PICTURE IS YOUR BEST GUIDE.

WHEN YOU DIE, YOUR MEMORIES DIE WITH YOU. WRITE THEM DOWN TO SHARE WITH YOUR LOVED ONES SO THEY CAN CARRY THEM ON.

THE PEOPLE WHO ARE THE HARDEST
TO LOVE ARE USUALLY THE ONES WHO
LONG FOR LOVE THE MOST.

WHEN YOU DO A FAVOR FOR SOMEONE,
NEVER EXPECT ANYTHING IN RETURN.
WHAT GOES AROUND, COMES AROUND.

IT'S WORTHWHILE TO PUSH
BOUNDARIES, BUT IT'S MORE
IMPORTANT NOT TO CROSS THEM.

TO CRAVE IS TO DENY HAPPINESS.

ALWAYS BE YOURSELF. THAT WAY YOU'RE IN CHARGE OF YOUR OWN DESTINY. NEVER LEAVE YOUR DESTINY UP TO OTHERS.

YOU HAVE A SMALLER PART THAN YOU THINK WHEN IT COMES TO RAISING YOUR CHILDREN WHEN COMPARED WITH THEIR PEER INFLUENCE AND THEIR ENVIRONMENT. MAXIMIZE YOUR TIME AND POSITIVE INFLUENCE THAT YOU HAVE WITH YOUR KIDS.

LOOKING FOR A GEOGRAPHICAL FIX
TO YOUR PROBLEMS IS NEVER THE
ANSWER. SOLVE YOUR PROBLEMS IN
SITU. OTHERWISE, YOUR PROBLEMS
WILL FOLLOW YOU EVERYWHERE.

SOMETIMES TAKING A TRIP TO NOWHERE IS EXACTLY WHAT THE DOCTOR ORDERED.

BEING MISUNDERSTOOD IS THE FATE OF MOST GENIUSES.

WHEN YOU HAVE A FORCEFUL VOICE, ALWAYS BE SURE TO COMPLEMENT IT WITH A SMILE.

**LOVE IS THE SOIL FOR GROWTH.
WITHOUT SOIL, NOTHING GROWS.**

PEOPLE LIKE TO TELL YOU WHAT'S
GOOD FOR YOU. THEY DON'T WANT
YOU TO FIND YOUR OWN ANSWERS.
THEY WANT YOU TO BELIEVE THEIRS.

ONE OF THE SECRETS TO HAPPINESS IS NOT FOUND IN SEEKING MORE, BUT IN LEARNING HOW TO ENJOY LESS.

TO BE AUTHENTIC MEANS TO BE YOUR OWN AUTHOR.

TO LIVE A LIFE FULL OF TRIALS AND TRIBULATIONS IS MUCH MORE SATISFYING THAN TO LIVE NO LIFE AT ALL.

**OLD HABITS DIE HARD, BUT YOU
HAVE THE ABILITY TO CHANGE THEM.**

BEING ABLE TO TAKE NAPS IS A SKILL THAT MOST PEOPLE DON'T HAVE. IF YOU CAN MASTER THAT SKILL, YOU WILL HAVE THE ABILITY TO WAKE UP BRIGHT EYED AND BUSHY-TAILED LIKE IT'S A NEW DAY WHENEVER YOU WANT.

IF YOU BLAME EVERYTHING ABOUT YOURSELF ON YOUR GENES, YOU'LL NEVER CHANGE.

THE DIFFERENCE BETWEEN BEING A LEADER AND BEING A FOLLOWER IS HAVING THE COURAGE TO CHOOSE TO LEAD.

ONCE YOU LET GO OF WHAT'S
WORRYING YOU, YOUR EYES AND EARS
OPEN WIDER, AND THE WORLD IS
YOUR TEACHER.

KNOWLEDGE HAS A FUNNY WAY OF DAMPENING FEAR. THE UNKNOWN CAN BE FRIGHTENING.

WHEN YOU USE TOO MANY WORDS TO EXPRESS YOURSELF, YOU RUN THE RISK OF YOUR MESSAGE LOSING ITS MEANING.

KIDS ARE LIKE CATS. IF YOU CHASE
THEM, THEY WILL EITHER HISS AT
YOU OR RUN AWAY. LET YOUR KIDS
COME TO YOU.

BIG THINGS MATTER IN RELATIONSHIPS, BUT IT'S THE LITTLE THINGS THAT MATTER THE MOST.

ANY LIE BREAKS TRUST, AND TRUST
IS VERY DIFFICULT TO REBUILD.
ALWAYS BE HONEST AND DEAL WITH
THE CONSEQUENCES.

SOCIETAL STANDARDS TODAY ARE
BASED ON THE CULMINATION OF
PEOPLE'S IDEALS AND ACTIONS
THOUGHOUT THOUSANDS OF YEARS.
YOU DON'T HAVE TO ACCEPT
SOCIETY'S EXPECTATIONS; YOU JUST
HAVE TO EXIST ALONGSIDE THEM.
LIVE BY YOUR OWN GOOD STANDARDS.

TAKE ALL THINGS IN STRIDE. THAT'S THE ONLY WAY TO MAINTAIN YOUR PATH.

**ALWAYS KNOW ALL OF THE FACTS
BEFORE YOU FORM AN OPINION.**

DON'T BE A SLAVE TO MONEY. AS LONG
AS YOU HAVE ENOUGH TO SURVIVE
COMFORTABLY, YOU'LL HAVE ALL
THAT YOU NEED TO LIVE A GOOD LIFE.

SETTING UNREALISTIC EXPECTATIONS
INEVITABLY LEADS TO
DISAPPOINTMENT. SEE THE BIG
PICTURE AND BE REALISTIC.

DON'T FEAR FAILURE. CHALLENGE IT.

WHEN YOUR SPOUSE GETS UPSET,
JUST REMEMBER THAT SAYING A
SIMPLE, "CALM DOWN" IN A
SOOTHING VOICE IS ALL THAT IT
TAKES TO GET THEM MORE ANGRY.

**NOBODY'S PERFECT. THEY CRUCIFIED
THE LAST PERFECT PERSON.**

YOU NEED TO LEARN TO GET A
LICENSE IN YOUR FIELD. YOU THEN
NEED TO WORK IN YOUR FIELD TO
LEARN.

THE ONLY PEOPLE WHO CAN BETRAY YOU ARE THE ONES THAT YOU TRUST.

NEVER BE AFRAID TO ASK FOR HELP
WHEN YOU NEED IT, BUT DON'T ASK
FOR HELP JUST BECAUSE YOU WANT
IT.

ALWAYS PLAN FOR THE WORST AND HOPE FOR THE BEST.

PATIENCE IS THE KEY TO UNDERSTANDING.

NO MATTER WHAT THE CIRCUMSTANCES ARE, YOU ALWAYS HAVE THE FREEDOM TO CHOOSE YOUR OWN ATTITUDE.

IT TAKES A VERY STRONG AND
HONEST PERSON TO SAY THE WORDS,
"I DON'T KNOW."

TRUSTING YOUR INSTINCT WHEN
MAKING DECISIONS MAY LEAD TO
REGRET ON OCCASION. BUT NOT EVER
TRUSTING YOUR GUT WILL LEAD TO A
LIFETIME OF REGRET.

PRECONCEIVED NOTIONS INEVITABLY LEAD TO A CONFUSED PERSPECTIVE.

YOUR NATURE IS THE FOUNDATION
FOR WHO YOU ARE. NURTURE AND
LIFE'S EXPERIENCES DECIDE THE
REST.

IF YOU ALWAYS INSIST THAT YOU'RE RIGHT ABOUT EVERYTHING, YOU NOT ONLY ANNOY THE PEOPLE AROUND YOU, BUT YOU ALSO CLOSE THE DOOR ON YOUR ABILITY TO LEARN.

KNOWLEDGE REQUIRES AN
UNDERSTANDING. WISDOM REQUIRES
A LIFETIME OF EXPERIENCE.

STONEWALLING WILL GET YOU NOWHERE. EITHER EMBRACE COMMUNICATION OR CHOOSE TO MOVE ON.

IF YOU RESPECT SOMEONE, YOU RESPECT THEIR TIME. NOT ONE PERSON'S TIME IS MORE IMPORTANT THAN SOMEONE ELSES'.

TAKING ACCOUNTABILITY FOR YOUR
ACTIONS IS SOMETHING THAT IS
BECOMING EXTINCT IN TODAY'S
WORLD. TAKING ACCOUNTABILITY IS
ANALOGOUS TO 'GRABBING THE BULL
BY THE HORNS.'

THOSE WHO ARE WILLING TO TAKE RISKS ARE THOSE WHO ARE ALSO GOOD AT SOLVING PROBLEMS ON THE SPOT.

'BEFORE I CRITICIZE A MAN, I FIRST LIKE TO WALK A MILE IN HIS SHOES. SO THAT WAY, WHEN I'M READY TO CRITICIZE HIM, I'M A MILE AWAY, AND I HAVE HIS SHOES.', -JACK HANDY

THE END

Made in the USA
Monee, IL
14 January 2024

50803696R10062